T0208264

THE UNTOLD EXPLOITATION OF RIDESHARE
DRIVERS AND RIDERS

THE NEW SLAVE LABOR MARKET POLICIES

GEORGE INUEN

authorHOUSE®

AuthorHouse™
1663 Liberty Drive
Bloomington, IN 47403
www.authorhouse.com
Phone: 833-262-8899

Published by AuthorHouse 03/14/2023

ISBN: 979-8-8230-0366-7 (sc)
ISBN: 979-8-8230-0365-0 (hc)
ISBN: 979-8-8230-0364-3 (e)

Library of Congress Control Number: 2023905018

Print information available on the last page.

CONTENTS

ACKNOWLEDGMENTS

This book is dedicated to rideshare drivers fighting for their rights and the dignity they deserve as independent contractors on digital taxi platforms that have disingenuously stripped them of those rights.

Also, a warm thanks to family members for their contributions and support.

My thanks to Mr. Okon Anwanane, aka the Megastar, and Mr. Godwin Ebong for their useful suggestions and contributions.

A special thanks to the dedicated staff of AuthorHouse for making the publication of this book possible.

INTRODUCTION

I feel that I have something of a calling to write about the rideshare drivers' vulnerability to exploitation and abuse in the absence of any guidelines or legal framework for protection. This book is written within the context of false promises of economic prosperity and good quality of life for rideshare drivers made by digital taxi platforms on launching. In fact, they delivered quite the opposite: economic hardship, poverty, and labor conditions reminiscent of the slavery era.

This book should be viewed within the context of labor-market economic policies of exploitation that aggravate rather than ameliorate financial hardships of drivers on digital taxi platforms. It wouldn't make much sense to talk about exploitation and slave wages in abstract without identifying such key factors as lack of a framework of protection for drivers and inaction on the part of lawmakers. These create an opportunity for rideshare digital taxi platforms to extort money from drivers and riders through manipulation of commissions, surge pricing, and cancellation fees.

Some of these factors, including drivers' inability to exercise their bargaining power collectively, are an affront to the claim of an economic model of prosperity and upward mobility. Those drivers with work experience as independent contractors on both regular taxi platforms and digital platforms are well positioned to expound on the difference.

Oftentimes when a scheme of exploitation and enslavement are exposed, we hear sarcastic apologies asking people to forget about "the mistakes we made in the past and look at what we are doing now and what we will do in the future"—all intended to hide the truth about a predatory algorithm pay structure designed to exploit drivers ruthlessly for corporate wealth creation. If and when rideshare drivers become fed up with slave wages and summon up the courage to say enough is enough, their prospects are bleak. Rideshare drivers are simply the chattel of rideshare companies, with no power whatsoever to negotiate for their rights as independent contractors, and no right to negotiate for any other benefits in a business they are an integral part of.

Rideshare companies treat drivers as slaves, with no compensatory benefits and no power to determine or negotiate the worth of their labor for trips, irrespective of the fare the company collects from riders. Lack of an established regulatory standard of earnings per mile and any channel for drivers to redress the unjust financial exploitation and abuse has undoubtedly empowered digital taxi companies to treat drivers on their platforms as slave laborers.

For every dollar of a rider's fare, Uber, for example, pockets sixty cents or more—that's at least 60 percent. Compare that to oil companies, which do not make such a whopping percentage per barrel of oil. In 2021, for example, oil prices averaged $71 dollars a barrel, with an expected profit projection of at least $15 dollars or about 21.1% a barrel, whether that oil was refined into gasoline, jet fuel, or home heating oil, among other options.

This is what rideshare companies are doing now. In the future, riders' fares will be far higher, and drivers' earnings will be fiendishly slashed, with eighty cents of every dollar of a rider's fare going into the company's pocket at the expense of struggling drivers trying to make a living while incurring huge expenses on a daily basis. Notice here that what they are doing now and what they will do in the future precludes a pay structure aimed at improving the earnings and benefits of drivers to enhance economic prosperity.

The issue of paying drivers slave wages has always been carefully dodged, with window-dressing diversionary answers to fool the public. When the take rate is successfully reversed—drivers earning 25 percent or less of a rider's fare and rideshare companies taking 75 percent or more—the companies' future will be bright and extremely profitable. When that goal is achieved, the profits of oil and other big companies will simply be a drop in the ocean in comparison.

This book focuses on the way rideshare companies use their platforms to exploit, manipulate, cheat, control, and humiliate drivers whose livelihoods depend on the transportation business. You will learn about a pay structure for drivers that guarantees rideshare companies retain a far bigger share of a rider's fare through unfair price-fixing whenever it serves their interest most, and above all reneging on a 25 percent commission they have no intention of adhering to. They also use surge pricing to more than double the fare riders pay, which would be an illegal and unacceptable practice for traditional transportation businesses—such as regular taxis, limousines, and shuttle buses—even when there is a major event that brings hundreds of people into a city.

Studies have shown that the price-surging scheme hardly benefits drivers.[1] Traditional transportation businesses involved in surge pricing would either pay fines or lose their license to operate and would certainly fall in the category of price-gougers. So, what gives one company an edge over another in the same type of business, and what is the rationale behind this disparity?

The lack of a regulatory framework to protect drivers from exploitation and abuse has opened the gateway to recreate the master-slave relationship of an earlier era. Crucial to the successful operation of ridesharing companies are drivers who bear the brunt of financial costs associated with the taxi transportation business but cannot negotiate for a fair share of the rider's fare because rideshare companies exercise complete authority and control over drivers, as did slave-masters over their slaves.

To maintain the status quo, rideshare companies have indefatigably fought against the establishment of a pricing model that guarantees a livable take-home pay for drivers rather than slave wages that do nothing but create a wide income inequality gap. The riders may gain a little savings except

---

[1] . Dhruv Mehrotra and Aaron Gordon, "Uber And Lyft Take a Lot More from Drivers Than They Say," Jalopnik (August 26, 2019).

during the surge pricing period. The discounted fare that gives financial relief to a rider actually comes at the expense of the earnings drivers receive for their labor, determined unilaterally by rideshare companies that leave no options whatsoever for drivers to negotiate for fare adjustment.

The question is: Who is paying the price to sustain the digital taxi business? Undoubtedly the drivers, whose earnings per trip are determined unilaterally by the rideshare companies. At the end of the day, this earning model does not provide a livable take-home income to enable drivers to meet financial obligations, such as car notes, insurance, maintenance, car depreciation, mortgage, rent, and putting food on the table for the family.

Considering the fact that the rider's fare is discounted and the rideshare companies pocket a high percentage of the already discounted fare—55 percent or even more— the driver must use the rest to cover all associated operating costs. These wages will give the reader an insight into what a rideshare driver whose only source of income derives from the transportation business goes through every day to make ends meet. Drivers put in many hours behind the wheel, incur huge expenses associated with running and maintaining a vehicle, and end up making less than a minimum wage by far.

The concept of a minimum wage, irrespective of the type of work, is to provide workers with at least the minimum amount needed to provide food, clothing, and shelter for themselves and their families. In reality, what rideshare drivers get out of their labor and investment is subsistence wages that offer no savings to replace their vehicle when the need arises, and no savings to fall back on in case of medical emergencies.

In truth, the purported commission or *take rate* only serves to mask these companies' exploitative practices through all kinds of unrestrained manipulations. Despite protests by labor unions and taxi companies against the slave wages and abuse rideshare drivers are subjected to, nothing whatsoever has been done by those in authority to ensure a fair distribution of income on taxi digital platforms poised to create a slave-labor market without any type of accountability or regulatory control.

The inaction on the part of transportation regulators and lawmakers amounts to a complete sell-out of rideshare drivers, allowing rideshare companies to exploit, cheat, and abuse them. One of the objectives of consumer protection laws is to prevent dangerous and unethical business practices against workers. The powerful taking undue advantage of the weak is what gave rise to all kinds of laws enacted by federal and state governments in the first place. Those in positions of authority should take a deeper look at the modus operandi of rideshare companies in relation to the financial exploitation of drivers and extortion of money from riders in the name of surge pricing.

A careful examination of their motto, objective, vision, and lack of transparency finds that it is driven by sheer greed, exploitation, and enslavement of those desperately trying to put food on their tables, of those trying to have a roof over their heads, of those trying to stay afloat in an abyss of craziness.

We are gradually heading into a new wave of exploitation and slavery in the name of an innovative transport platform with almost all the attributes of slave-masters of the past centuries. It's a rebirth of the master-slave relationship, an unconscionable exploitation and abuse of a targeted group. Their voices and cries for fairness and justice have been long been ignored by those who should know better.

With their unlimited power, rideshare companies abuse their drivers without whips or chains. Yet it is essentially a modern-day platform of slavery, in which drivers who give legitimacy and sustainability to the companies' business operations are stripped of their independent contractor rights and benefits. Rideshare businesses involve three parties: a rider who pays a discounted fare below regular taxi rates, a rideshare company that retains the maximum amount possible of that fare, and the driver who receives the least earning out of it and is consequently robbed of the revenue that should go to him.

CHAPTER 1

The Secret Behind the Mottos and Objectives of Rideshare Companies

I'd like to start this chapter by highlighting the deceptive mottos and objectives of two popular rideshare companies, Uber and Lyft.

Uber says, "It is our goal to create a workplace that is inclusive and reflects the diversity of the cities we serve—where everyone can be their authentic self." Its mission is "Transportation as reliable as running water, everywhere for everyone."

Lyft describes its mission as "Improving people's lives with the world's best transportation. Ride by ride, we are changing the way our world works. We imagine a world where cities feel small again ..." The company's values are:

- Be yourself
- Uplift others
- Make it happen

As lofty and laudable as these goals are, beneath all of their bluster is a secret agenda that is driven by greed and exploitation of the immigrants, retirees, and people of color who constitute their core labor force and whose only source of income is the transportation business. In truth, the companies have taken bread from the mouths of these drivers through lies and deception, with rosy visions of upward mobility and economic freedom.

Spending thousands of dollars to purchase vehicles that may fall into the category of UberX, Uber Pro, and what have you, to earn on the average sixty-five cents per mile is creating an economic model in which the rich get richer and the poor get poorer. The idea imbedded in the rideshare companies' mission is creating a utopian world where anything you need is delivered with the press of a button. For a discounted transportation platform that registers no single car in the company's business name, incurs no costs associated with running a taxi business, but has disgruntled exploited drivers, how practical is it to translate these utopian models to deal with the inherent transportation problems in the real world?

The truth is that Uber, Lyft, and other rideshare companies have discovered an unprotected gold mine of a labor force to dig into and exploit, unrestrained, for corporate wealth creation. The payoff is so great that Uber, Lyft, and other rideshare companies are willing to do anything to maintain absolute control of this gold mine of labor. It's comparable to the gold rush.

Demographically, drivers of rideshare companies are overwhelmingly people of color, retirees, and immigrants facing daunting challenges. This is where the gold mine of labor exploitation lies. This is one of the reasons rideshare companies have mounted aggressive efforts, spending millions of dollars by way of campaign contributions and lobbying, along with false projections of drivers' earnings, to derail any legal framework of protection for the drivers in order to monopolize, control, and maintain this slave-labor market unchecked and unregulated.

These rideshare platforms see drivers as indispensable tools for corporate growth and wealth creation. They will do anything and everything, stop at nothing, employ all kinds psychological tricks of intimidation to ensure that anyone in this pool of laborers who cries foul over unfair and unethical practices and abuses is completely submerged under the ocean. The relationship between rideshare companies and drivers is one in which the former has complete authority and control over the latter in terms of bargaining power and wages. These companies have absolved themselves of most, if not all, financial burden and obligation associated with running a transportation business and shifted those responsibilities to drivers without any type of livable wages, compensation, and benefits in return.

Amazingly, Uber and other rideshare platforms pretend that these costs do not exist by pocketing a large percentage of riders' fares through such methods as service charges—a variable fee Uber charges a driver for every trip serviced (equivalent to selling trips)—and a variable booking fee that can be as high as airline booking fees. They then apply a commission rate quite above the promised 25 percent of the remainder to determine the driver's pay.

Note here that all fees and commissions are variable, and whatever amount Uber takes for its fees and commission for any given trip is not subject to challenge or review. Through this scheme, Uber and other rideshare companies can take as much of the rider's fare as they want, leaving as little as they can for the driver.

It would be absurd to believe that rideshare companies are not aware of the high cost of purchasing and maintaining a vehicle for a transportation business, especially in a situation that requires putting hundreds of miles a day on the odometer. The fact is, they don't care. What matters is how much they can milk out of drivers to create unfathomable wealth for themselves. Otherwise, how, in good conscience and fairness, would they expect a payment of fifty-five to sixty-five cents a mile to cover all these costs and take-home wages? This is a deliberate, unconscionable scheme of exploitation.

The misleading figures of driver earnings do not take into account car notes, insurance, maintenance, depreciation, gas, and frequent oil changes, all borne by drivers, even as gas and spare-parts prices have skyrocketed. What is the motive behind riders' fares going up while, at the same time, drivers' earnings are ruthlessly slashed? Absolute exploitation, echoed in utterances such as "We pay because we can."

This statement is the closest they have come to admitting they are exploiting drivers with slave wages, with pride. It's a slap in the face for the drivers. When gas prices really skyrocketed, the most drivers got was an addition of a paltry fifty-five-cent fuel surcharge irrespective of the distance, and a noticeable decrease in earnings per mile.

Uber has often claimed that its take rate is 25 percent, but study after study has shown this to be false.[2] Uber's policy of unilaterally determining a driver's earning for a trip is a hidden secret agenda of extortion designed to manipulate the maximum amount of the riders' fare going into its pocket first. For sure this policy neither helps a driver cover his expenses nor guarantees meaningful take-home pay after expenses.

Uber determines the booking fee, which is a percentage of the total fare a rider pays for a trip. Astonishingly, the booking fee can be as high as that of an airline booking fee, even though it is for a four-wheel-drive trip. Booking fees and service charges go straight to Uber before the commission or questionable take rate of 25 percent is deducted from whatever remains. Higher booking fees mean Uber's effective commission is also higher, which is one of the methods systematically employed to rob drivers of their fair earnings.

Upon launching, Uber proclaimed itself "nothing more than a neutral technological platform, designed simply to enable drivers and passengers to transact the business of transportation." This is false, because Uber retains control over the operation as a whole. There is an imbedded secret scheme of extortion here,

---

2 . David Mamaril Horowitz, "As Rideshare Prices Skyrocket, Uber and Lyft Take a Bigger Bite of the Pie," *Mission Local* (July 15, 2021), https://missionlocal.org/2021/07/as-rideshare-prices-skyrocket-uber-and-lyft-take-a-bigger-bite-of-the-pie/.

because the interaction with a rider and the earnings of a driver are totally dictated by Uber, contrary to the above proclamation.

As a matter of fact, price-fixing is one of the tools Uber uses to cheat and extort money from drivers. Drivers cannot negotiate for a fair share of the rider's fare or any type of earning adjustment; it's a take-it-or-leave-it deal. Of all the updates Uber claims to display on its app to help drivers make a decision, the one feature that has remained shrouded in secrecy is its total commission of a rider's fare as a function of the earning of a driver for a given trip.

Uber has always hidden the statistical data that as prices of every conceivable product have skyrocketed, it is charging riders more and still offering, on the average, sixty-five cents a mile to drivers. A ride from downtown Houston to George Bush International Airport, for example, is twenty-two miles or more, depending on the pickup location. Uber charged a customer $34 and paid the driver $12.86. What justifies paying a driver a slave-labor earning of $12.86 while Uber pockets $21.14 just for dispatching a trip, other than taking undue advantage, just because you can?

This, by any standard, is an economic model designed to create unlimited wealth for Uber while driving drivers into abject poverty. Remember that transportation is the only source of income for the majority of these drivers. If your conscience tells you that something is not right based on some of the statistical facts above, then you have to wonder how forthright and honest Uber is in regard to its booking fee, service fee, and take rate relative to drivers' earnings.

Silence is complicity, and there comes a time when silence becomes a crime. There is a growing movement of opposition to the Uber economy; many believe is no different from the colonial model of slavery. Nobody wants to reset the clock to that painful and agonizing era. It took centuries of fight by enlightened people of good will and courage to end the inhumane exploitation of the weak by the powerful, and you can be a part of that history now by speaking out loudly against this new wave of exploitation targeting drivers on their platform. The annals of history will inscribe your name among those who fought to end injustice in order to bring about peace and economic prosperity to humanity in general. History will remember you forever.

As Martin Luther King once said, "There comes a time when people get tired of being trampled over by the iron feet of oppression, there comes a time, my friends, when people get tired of being plunged across the abyss of humiliation, where they experience the bleakness of nagging despair." Some of the reasons rideshare drivers protest and go on strikes nationally and globally, is summarized in the above excerpt.

The truth is, Uber has never been forthright in its apps algorithm design, which lacks transparency relevant to the earnings of Uber drivers and surge pricing. Uber and other rideshare companies' policies are not designed for the economic prosperity and upward mobility of the drivers but for exploiting and reducing them to perpetual servitude, orbiting around that cycle of complete hopelessness, frustration, and poverty. Purchasing a vehicle for a transportation business is an investment, and if the returns are constantly negative, then the investor (the driver) is obviously left to writhe in the pain of financial losses. He has to start over, looking for someone to finance another vehicle purchase with the belief that things will probably get better. But they never will under the current dispensation, and so the repetition of the vicious cycle of losses continues, which is one of the ways many rideshare drivers are crippled financially, resulting in suicides and homelessness.

Before brushing this off, consider the quantitative difference in income for a driver. The difference in dollar amount Uber and other rideshare companies craftily dupe drivers into—through deceptive manipulation of their commission, booking, and service fees—would certainly go a long way toward alleviating the financial burdens they incur and, perhaps, add a little more to bolster their take-home wages. Using their financial influence and connections to derail a pay-structure framework that would uplift drivers financially, rideshare companies have set a continuum of charges ranging from the minimum to the very highest to manipulate and cheat drivers of their fair share of the fare.

The Uber app design and deployment, for example, allows it to produce a management labor force that monitors driver activity on its platform once the driver is online. This constant monitoring of the driver's activities can result in a driver being deactivated or cancelled based on subjective complaints rather than objective evidence. Algorithm management really constrains worker autonomy through surveillance and ranking systems that measure individual performance, and a customer rating that may form the basis of deactivating a driver.

While Uber's contract with its "partners" outlines (section 4.1) that the fare Uber sets is a "recommended" amount (drivers technically have the right to charge less, but not more, than the pre-arranged fare), there is no way for drivers to actually negotiate the fare within the Uber app. Before, when a driver accepted a trip, he did not know how much he was going to earn for the trip; it was entirely up to Uber to pay a driver any amount as his earning, and the driver could not negotiate for more. Recently, Uber, has updated its app algorithm to show the distance to a pickup location, the distance to a drop-off location, and the amount a driver earns for the trip, which has no correlation whatsoever to the rider's fare. Rather, a driver's earning is the leftover after all sorts of manipulation from booking fees, service charges, and take rate as Uber sees fit. This cannot be challenged or reviewed by anyone as a violation of a wage earning far below the federal minimum wage standardized and fitting within the framework of slave wages.

So, for example, if Uber charges a rider $50 and offers the driver $19 or less, there is absolutely nothing a driver can do to get a fair fare-adjustment consideration. It is what it is, and if this is not a rebirth of the slave-master model of exploitation and abuse of the past centuries, I don't know what is. The same is true of tips riders give to a driver. It is difficult to know the correct tip amount. Tip amounts are displayed in the inbox with faint details, and this is also true with the delivery services. There are a lot of complaints of pilfering of tips riders give to drivers.

Consider a rider adding a tip of five dollars or ten dollars to a driver. Uber shows a tip of two dollars and five dollars respectively. There is absolutely no way of knowing the correct tip amount. Drivers can send a note of thanks to the rider, but the text of the note is controlled and transmitted by Uber through its text messages app.

When it comes to a driver's earning for any given trip, the truth is that Uber is the sole decider. It does not take a mathematical genius to see how Uber and other rideshare companies have methodically used their platform algorithms to exploit and cheat drivers. When it comes to money, everything is shrouded in secrecy. Fairness and transparency are thrown to the wind.

From the inception of the taxi business, local and federal regulators put in place laws and regulations to protect the drivers, as independent contractors, from abuse and exploitation by powerful taxi companies. Such laws and regulations are completely nonexistent in the digital taxi business, which is why these companies have successfully turned their platforms to a model of slavery and exploitation.

Essentially, Uber is in the seat of the prosecutor and the judge. The driver is its pawn. It offers slave-wage earnings to drivers without any consideration; inflicts financial pain and suffering at will; and subjects drivers to its whims and caprices. It's a medieval battleground, to say the least.

The astonishing aspect of the rideshare companies' policies is their manipulative power and ability to evade local, state, and even federal regulatory guidelines in the commercial taxi business by wearing a different mask but rendering the same service. Uber, for example, has the full power to unilaterally set and change the fares passengers pay, booking fees, service charges, and commission rates to minimize drivers' earnings to any level unhindered. How long will these drivers remain oppressed and exploited?

One thing is obvious: if nothing is done to institute a legal framework to minimize financial exploitation and abuse of drivers, it will take a considerable amount of effort to correct the unrealistic algorithm pay structure designed purely to take undue advantage of drivers. The common denominator here is lack of regulation and accountability. The unbridled power to pay slave wages is one of the reasons Uber and other rideshare companies have been able to use their platforms to treat drivers like rats in a cage.

CHAPTER 2

The Role of Drivers in the Success of Rideshare Companies

Rideshare companies have no assets related to their core business. They depend on drivers who use their own vehicles or rent vehicles from affiliated rental companies to operate under their banner, without which they would exist in name only.

Without any iota of doubt, drivers play a vital role in the operation and success of rideshare taxi businesses, and yet they are treated with contempt. The drivers are the ones who give legitimacy to the companies' successful business operations, take risks, and bear almost all the financial responsibilities and costs associated with the transportation business. In return, they are denied any right to an acceptable negotiated take rate (commission taken by the company) sanctioned by regulatory agencies and the federal department of transportation. Without this safeguard in place, rideshare drivers are forever doomed to be bullied.

It Is Never a Wise Idea to Allow a Fox to Guard a Henhouse

From the inception of the transportation business—taxis, limousines, etc.—the number-one attribute was providing service by dispatching a driver to pick up a customer at a location, no matter the platform used. Methods of trip-dispatching have varied over the years—voice, electronic, digital, apps. The bottom line has always been providing taxi service at the request of a customer. Service is contingent upon the availability of drivers in the vicinity of the pickup location—but more importantly, on the willingness of a driver to provide service to the customer.

In essence, a platform system employed in trip dispatching does not in any way guarantee instant service at the location. It only provides a network of connection with the parties involved: the rider, the driver, and the taxi company base.

What has noticeably changed, in the case of digital taxi services, is the automated vehicle dispatch and payment honoring system that allows the rider to create an account with a digital taxi company using a credit card, debit card, or any other method for upfront payment. Communication between a rider, a driver, and the company platform for trip dispatch existed in many forms before. For example, the company would inform the customer (rider) via phone call of a service car's approximate time of arrival, and on arrival, the driver or company would call the customer to confirm. Apps now perform basically the same function, and there is no justification whatsoever to deny drivers their independent contractors' gate-fee right for integrating different hardware and software application functionalities that have long existed, tailored to the companies' digital taxi application needs.

Even if Uber and other rideshare apps are new creations, the policy of holding drivers financially hostage or using them as commodities in trade for any reason is repulsive. These drivers have a right to make a fair and decent living for the many hours they put behind the wheel. Trip dispatch is trip dispatch, period. Just as they say in first-year accounting course (101), at the close of any business day, all banking transactions boil down to *debit* and *credit*. So no matter how this app system is camouflaged, painted, colored, or portrayed, the truth is that rideshare companies are in the business of dispatching trips just like regular taxi platforms.

In reality, the launching of Uber came with no hardware or software that was uniquely new or revolutionary; rather, the most important "innovation" has been the production of staggering levels of private wealth without any sustainable benefits for consumers (riders), drivers, and workers, or technical innovations that greatly increase productivity and improve the living standards of society in general. So far, no rideshare company has created an automated platform system that automatically creates service cars to service customers (riders). Distance and time are critical factors that determine the number of trips a driver can make and his earnings on, say, a shift.

Consider a scenario in which a driver in service with a rider gets stuck in traffic as a result of unforeseen circumstances, such as accidents, road construction, or traffic holdup. The app design and deployment offer little or no additional financial compensation for the time he spends in traffic. For one thing, the company has already taken its share of the rider's fare, so the time a driver spends stuck in traffic costs them nothing; it is only an added cost for the driver in terms of fewer trips and lower income.

This is one of the ways rideshare drivers suffer financial losses. In many instances, the amount a driver is paid for a trip is so low that it would cost a rider more money and more time riding a Metro bus that requires changing buses two or three times to get to the destination. Cases like this raise a question as to whether rideshare drivers are not operating at less than the fare a Metro or shuttle bus rider would pay for the same destination.

The Fight for Survival and the War Against Exploitation

Studies have shown that Uber and Lyft offload soft costs on drivers and communities. In an article on *TechCrunch*, Devin Coldeway writes: "As the average cost of a ride on Uber, Lyft and other 'rideshare' services has risen over the years, it's become clear these companies were never entirely forthright about their business models. Now a pair of studies suggests even the investor-subsidized prices don't tell the whole story, with costs being borne by drivers and communities."[3]

---

[3] . Devin Coldewey, "Studies Say Uber and Lyft Offload Soft Costs on Drivers and Communities," *TechCrunch* (October 8, 2021), https://

While Uber, Lyft and other rideshare platforms have launched a sustained campaign of cheap and affordable transport service, the question is, at whose financial expense and disadvantage? Who is the sacrificial lamb on the altar of an unregulated and unchecked transport business that retains 60 percent or more of a rider's fare without sweat? Who is exploiting and abusing whom?

As Emperor Haile Selassie of Ethiopia stated in an address in Addis Ababa in 1963, "Throughout history it has been the inaction of those who could have acted, the indifference of those who should have known better, the silence of the voice of justice when it mattered most, that has made it possible for evil to triumph." Joint protests and complaints by labor unions, labor organizers, and cab companies globally against an industry they say threatens their livelihoods and the well-being of consumers have resulted in little or no action to address and resolve the issue of exploitation and slave wages by those in a position to act.

Recently, rallies have taken place across several cities in the US. According to a report in *The Guardian* by Kari Paul:[4]

> Hundreds of Uber and Lyft drivers have joined other app-based workers across the US for a day-long strike to protest poor working conditions and demand the right to organize.

---

techcrunch.com/2021/10/08/studies-say-uber-and-lyft-offload-soft-costs-on-drivers-and-communities/.

[4] . Kari Paul, "Uber and Lyft Drivers Join Day-Long Strike Over Working Conditions," *The Guardian* (July 21, 2021), https://www.theguardian.com/technology/2021/jul/21/uber-lyft-drivers-strike-app-based-work-gig-economy.

The workers are calling for better wages and congressional support of the Pro Act, a bill that would provide protections for workers who attempt to unionize, including members of the gig economy. The bill has stalled indefinitely after passing in the US House in March.

"App-based workers are fed up with exploitation from big tech companies," said Eve Aruguete, a driver from Oakland and a member of organizing group Rideshare Drivers United. "Misclassification is like concrete, keeping us underground. The Pro Act is the hammer that will break that concrete, allowing app-based workers to organize." ...

"Without drivers, there is no Uber—without drivers there is no Lyft," said Eddy Hernandez, formerly a senior software engineer at Uber who quit because he disagreed with how the company treated drivers.

"Tech workers and drivers need to come together and demand the end to the second-hand class employment status that restricts workers from having the pay and dignity only some are afforded," he added.

During the protest, Paul reports, slogans such as "strike for dignity" and "Uber and Lyft are driving us into poverty" were a common sight.

These are a few samples of protests taking place in many cities across the US and other parts of the world. Despite protests against exploitation, lack of protection, and the inherent features of these apps that make it easy for companies to cheat drivers of their fair share of rider's fare based on the company's take-rate settings, no action has been taken to rectify the situation by those who should act to ensure fairness.

The key question relating to the inaction on the part of lawmakers is whether campaign contributions have dampened the voice of justice to the point where lawmakers can completely ignore the clarion call to act and save drivers from exploitation. There is a saying that "there is dignity in labor." Where is that dignity in slave wages that gradually and painfully drag drivers in the business to the abyss of frustration and economic despair?

Campaign Contributions, Lobbying: The Inhibitor

The following articles suggest some reasons why politicians may not be coming to drivers' rescue. From *Vice*, September 23, 2020:

Uber, Lyft Give California GOP Millions While Fighting Driver Reclassification

The Yes on Proposition 22 gave $2 million to the California Republican Party last Friday.

By Edward Ongweso Jr
The Yes on Proposition 22 campaign—a ballot initiative bankrolled by Uber, Lyft, DoorDash,

Instacart, and Postmates to permanently protect themselves from reclassifying California drivers as employees—has donated $2 million to California's Republican Party.

The revelation was posted to Twitter on Monday by KPFA Radio reporter Ariel Boone. The donation was made on Friday, with additional contributions made exclusively to Ventura County and Santa Clara County Republican parties for an additional $20,000 and $2,593.15, respectively.

According to campaign finance records, the companies have contributed $184.3 million to the Yes on Proposition 22 campaign's war chest as of September 18. In a deep dive into the campaign's advertising operations, Darak Kerr of CNET found it had already spent millions on digital advertising, but that was likely only "a small fraction" of what would be spent on television advertisement. Here lies another way the campaign's money is being redirected to the GOP: consulting groups and lobbyists.

The Chris Mottola Consulting—founded by a former GOP operative and responsible for multiple ad campaigns for prominent GOP politicians—has helped craft multiple ads for the Yes on Prop 22 campaign. According to its website, advertisements that "tell the story of victims, villains, heroes and actions." Uber and

Lyft have also deployed a record number of lobbyists this year, many of whom have worked for prominent Republican lawmakers.

Generally, Democrats have been publicly supportive of California's Assembly Bill 5, which Proposition 22 seeks to exempt gig companies from complying with, while the GOP has vocally opposed it.

During the Democratic nomination race, prominent candidates including Senators Bernie Sanders, Elizabeth Warren, and Kamala Harris (whose brother-in-law Tony West is Uber's general counsel), expressed support for Assembly Bill 5h. After reluctant support for protesting ride-hail drivers, Democratic presidential nominee Joe Biden came around to supporting AB5.

Assembly Bill 5 has been regarded much more coldly by the GOP, however, especially by prominent figures such as Senator Ted Cruz, who attacked AB5 as part of a "daily war on jobs," and Representative Dan Crenshaw, who pointed at the bill as proof that "Republicans are the party of Uber" while "Democrats are the party of taxi cab unions."

"It was only a matter of time before they embraced the political party [that] wants what they want," Edan Alva, a ride-hail driver and organizer with driver advocacy group Gig Workers

Rising. "They'll do anything to protect their wage theft long enough to find a way to profit from it. Donating to the GOP hurts workers and drivers, but that's what they've been doing all along."

By comparison, the No on Proposition 22 campaign—financed largely by driver advocacy groups and unions—has raised a comparatively humble $5.6 million. To make up for the fact that they have almost 33 times less money than the gig company campaign, drivers have relied on generating attention through protests, press conferences, and actions meant to raise awareness of driver misclassification, poor working conditions in the industry, and exploitative labor practices.

"Early on during this crisis, I had to work even when I was sick. Even then, that was not enough and I almost found myself without a roof over my head," Alva said. "That is what these people are spending millions to defend. Not making sure we are safe, secure, well-paid, or have benefits, but whether we can help them one day make money. They won't stop with our industry. They'll spread this to every industry if they can."[5]

---

[5] . https://www.vice.com/en/article/qj4q7p/uber-lyft-give-california-gop-millions-while-fighting-driver-reclassification

From *TechCrunch*, June 2, 2021:

Rideshare drivers gather in NYC in hopes of unionizing.

Drivers protest outside of Uber's Queens offices ahead of a proposed state bill

Brian Heater

Protesters gathered in bright red t-shirt and matching masks bearing the independent Drivers Guild logo. Placards bearing slogans like "Freeze Hiring, Reactive Workers Now!" and "Unlock Uber" were being handed out at a table toward the entrance. What the gathering lacked in sheer numbers, it made up with enthusiasm.

A wide range of speakers approached the podium—IDG members, drivers, local and prospective politicians. Nearly every speech was followed by a spirited call and response from the crowd, culminating in pro-union chants. ...

The concerns of gig workers are nothing new, of course, but today's crowd gathered in Long Island City, Queens to add support to a proposed bill currently making its way through the state legislature in Albany. The legislation is designed to make it easy for gig economy workers in the state to unionize.

"Currently, the gig workers have no voice in their workplace. No voice to negotiate pay or benefits of workplace policies," bill sponsor state Sen. Diane Savino of Staten Island explained in a recent interview. "And I have been talking about this issue for several years now. The world of work is changing, and labor law has not caught up to technology and how it has changed the world of work."

Such legislation would have a profound impact on not just ride-hailing apps like Uber and Lyft, but also a wide range of gig economy jobs, including food delivery services like Seamless. ...

The rise of the gig economy has brought a number of key questions relating to the connection between worker protections and employee status to the fore.

What seems clear across the board, however, is that these drivers—and other gig economy workers—are seeking what, in many other industries, have become fairly fundamental protections. Of late, unionization has become a major talking point for blue and white-collar workers alike. ...

Like those workers, the list of complaints among drivers is long. When a speaker at today's event asked the crowd how many in attendance had had their accounts deactivated, the response was overwhelming. Many believed the decisions were made arbitrarily.

"A lot of drivers are falsely being accused, deactivated, thrown out of all these rideshare companies that they invested so much money on," Ahmed said.

The Independent Drivers Guild—which organized today's event along with the NYC Rideshare Club and the Chinese Delivery Association—isn't mincing words.

"By helping drivers through deactivated systems, we realized only a true union can solve that problem," Aziz Bah, IDG organizing director, told TechCrunch. "We decided to unionize. We will let the companies know what our plans are. They had better be behind our proposal. Because this is no negotiation. If this is what drivers and delivery workers want, they had better be behind it." [6]

Globally, there has been massive protests against Uber, Lyft, and other rideshare companies' operations, questioning the company's lack of transparency, ethics, and concern for the social cost. Taxi industries have argued that ridesharing companies are illegal taxicab operations that take away their business. Some countries have fully or partially banned Uber from operating in those countries in recognition that Uber's platform does nothing more than enslave and exploit their citizens with slave wages.

CHAPTER 3

The Economic Institution of Rideshare Companies

Rideshare drivers are the economic institution of the rideshare companies, just as slaves were the economic institution of slave owners. Let me proffer a few reasons why this is true. Before I delve into it, be guided by this excerpt from one of Booker T. Washington's writings:

A lie doesn't become truth;
Wrong doesn't become right, and evil doesn't become good,
Just because it's accepted by a majority.

Now consider the economic entities at play in the rideshare taxi platform market:

- the rideshare company
- the riders
- the drivers—the ultimate instrument of delivery.

I will start with this assertion: Rideshare practice and policies, in relation to drivers, are relics of slave-wage practices using modern technology. All it takes is fair knowledge of drivers' earnings in relation to a rider's fare for a trip and the laughable defense of company executives when asked about the slave wages they offer drivers for their services: "We pay because we can, people are not forced to drive for us." It's quite easy to decipher their ulterior motive without lectures from experts to be convinced that the above assertion is an axiomatic truth.

Psychological manipulation, gamification, and other techniques unearthed by social science are applied to nudge drivers not only to act and behave in certain ways but accept and adapt to slave wages of sixty-five cents per mile or less as the norm. The push by the gig economy in collaboration with other household-name companies to introduce a bill known as the "worker flexibility and choice act," which would exempt virtually any American worker from minimum-wage and overtime protection, is further attestation to the above assertion.

It is worth noting here that the main focus of some of these application techniques is to dehumanize and exploit drivers on their platforms with a pay structure that can never benefit drivers financially in a way that will enhance economic prosperity and upward mobility. Suggestion from any quarter, including concerned lawmakers, to set a minimum earning per mile of $1.17 or more to enhance a livable wage is always met with fierce opposition conjoined with huge spending in campaign contributions and lobbying.

The rideshare company Uber is said to be the world's

largest transportation industry, yet it does not own a single vehicle related to the core of its business. It depends entirely on individuals who use their own vehicles, or on individuals who can afford to rent cars from rental companies affiliated with Uber or any other ride-hailing company. Through this scheme, rideshare companies are able to place most of the financial burden relating to the transportation business on their drivers, who have no rights and no voice to negotiate for any decent rate of earning per mile or even the implementation of the so-called "take rate" referred to as *commission*.

Discounted rides are only made possible by ruthlessly discounting the earnings of rideshare drivers. This in turn explicitly implies that drivers are the tools of sustaining and legitimizing the discounted platform whereby these companies are able to create immense wealth for themselves. The rideshare economy is no different from the colonial model of exploitation of workers, where hourly payment was the norm with no longer term of benefits, no annual bonuses, and above all no medical and pension benefits.

There are virtually no laws or regulations that protect drivers and their rights, and this gives rideshare companies the impetus to treat drivers heartlessly, exploiting and abusing them at will. It's a master-slave business relationship within a democratic setup, a taxi cab company wearing a different mask with unlimited power and flexibility to exploit drivers—and, at opportune times, riders. The strategy behind affordable rides is based on quantity (more is better). The company discounts fares to attract customers, and at the same time ruthlessly underpays drivers for any given trip. This may work well for Uber but it certainly does not for drivers who bear the brunt of financial costs associated with the taxi transportation business but have no right whatsoever to negotiate for a fair share of the rider's fare.

It appears that in its quest to destroy the taxi business and become the only cock to crow, the supply-and-demand equation and philosophy of that business was completely ignored. The ugly, exploitative, and abusive part is that underpaid drivers, not Uber, are the ones held hostage financially to sustain discounted fares while Uber reaps billions of dollars in profit out of this skewed deal. A driver's earnings per trip are at the discretion of Uber. Drivers cannot negotiate for decent pay and are not allowed to unionize. This opens the gateway for unlimited exploitation and abuse. These companies see drivers as a springboard to the "get rich quick" dream—an indispensable source of funds to be exploited by all means, and at all costs.

Consider, for example, driving four or more miles to pick up a passenger with a drop-off location ten or more miles away, and getting paid five or six dollars. You are looking at close to an hour of driving and about half a gallon of gas on this one trip. Realistically, the amount earned for this trip, after deducting gas money and other incidental costs of about $1.00, the driver's pay is a paltry $2.00 to $2.50. The guarantee offered to drivers in this setup is slave labor, not quality wages.

Uber has the prerogative to pay a driver whatever it wants. It pays fifty-five cents per mile, taking 55 percent of the rider's fare for itself. The ability to subject drivers to accept any pay it offers without any standardized framework, up to $1.20 per mile, rather than fifty-five cents per mile, is a bleeding wound to drivers.

The rideshare digital taxi business shifts the financial burden of running a taxi business, including car-note payments, insurance, repair, and maintenance—which traditional taxi companies used to incur—completely to their drivers, who they disingenuously classify as independent contractors without the benefit of the gate-fee rights of independent contractors working for non-digital taxi companies.

For one thing, if you set ridiculously low fares, own no vehicles, but rack in millions of dollars every day, it doesn't take a rocket scientist to figure out that somebody is indirectly subsidizing this. That subsidizer is unquestionably the exploited driver. Look at it from any angle, apply any logic you want, drivers are not only abused and exploited but are the human chattel of the rideshare companies. The companies have been able to subject drivers to their will.

So you don't think this is a philosophical or sentimental statement, I will give a few statistics in the coming chapters that will help you determine whether or not rideshare drivers are the economic institution of the rideshare companies, just as slaves were the economic institution of slave owners of past centuries. Even as gas prices have soared and drivers are struggling to make ends meet, Uber is capitalizing on the situation to exploit drivers ruthlessly, slashing their earnings to benefit itself financially, adding a paltry fifty-five-cent fuel surcharge without consideration to the economic realities, including spare parts, oil changes, and other car maintenance costs that are more expensive now than before. This is sad. These are modern-day dark days of slavery in disguise.

We know that fuel prices have skyrocketed. Fuel consumption is determined by mileage, not by the number of trips a driver makes. Paying fifty-five cents as a fuel subsidy irrespective of the trip distance is preposterous. To portray a good public image, Uber, for example, deceptively puts out an X-dollar-amount subsidy—such as $22 if a driver makes forty trips. The question is, how many miles does a driver cover in forty trips to earn the big gift of $22 from benevolent Uber? This is in line with its scheme of exploitation and is an insult to drivers.

Ever since the Uber algorithm was updated, this has been the pattern: lower pay for drivers, more money for Uber. The updated algorithm has made it easier to manipulate pay so that drivers earn less for the same-distance trips, and Uber widens its profit margin. As an example, for a trip from downtown Houston to George Bush International Airport, Uber used to pay between $16 and $17. With the new pay algorithm, coupled with the appetite to milk more money from drivers, Uber offers between $11 and $13 for the same trip. It's simple psychology: when the familiar chime of an incoming-trip offer comes on the phone, there will always be a driver desperate enough to accept any amount. It's not only taking undue advantage of the disadvantaged, it is a horrendous abuse of power.

The logic justifying the unfair scheme is that the distance and the rate offered for the trip are displayed on the screen to enable the driver make a decision as to whether to accept or reject the trip. Therefore, there can be no trip fare adjustment, period. But where is the correlation between Uber's claimed take rate of 25 percent in relation to the fare the rider is charged versus the amount a drive earns? None whatsoever. It's like, "Hey! Take it or not. We have many out there desperately in need of money."

This scheme deprives a driver of the right and benefit of being an independent contractor or an employee in a business environment where Uber decides how many hours a driver can work, determines how much he can earn per trip, suspends a driver temporary for rejecting trips he considers not worth his while, and schedules when his hard-earned money can be paid to his account. Meanwhile, the driver's earnings in Uber's business account is accruing interest for Uber while drivers wait for the scheduled payment date, unless there is an instant payment request, in which case a transfer fee is charged. This is the inconvenient truth of how Uber has meticulously, deceitfully manipulated drivers to create corporate wealth.

Independent contractor issues or clauses are nothing new in the taxi business. It is characterized by a gate-fee agreement that stipulates how much a driver pays per day for using the provider's platform. This setup allows drivers to keep their fares and tips. In the case of rideshare companies, this gate fee or commission has been split into service charge, booking fee, and take rate, after deducting the service and booking fees of the fare paid by a rider. Total commission or total take rate comprises booking fees, service fees, and commission as a percentage of a rider's fare, not as a complex matrix.

Uber's definition of a service charge is the fee drivers pay Uber, and it varies from trip to trip. It is the difference between what a rider pays and what a driver earns on a trip, excluding tips, tolls, and certain fees, taxes, and surcharges. Note here that it is the driver who sacrifices his vehicle to give legitimacy and sustainability to the platform. Instead of adding the service charge to the driver's earning to offset his insurance, car notes, maintenance, and depreciation costs, it charges the driver a fee for the service drivers render to promote and give credence to its platform. Without the service of these drivers, Uber's platform and other ride-hailing platforms would be a paper tiger and nothing more. Perhaps a week or even a few days down by these exploited drivers will prove the point without any iota of doubt.

Uber stipulates a booking fee of one dollar minimum and not exceeding ten dollars maximum of the rider's pay, a take rate of 25 percent and above after the service charge and the booking fee are subtracted from the rider's fare. Whatever amount of money Uber decides on as its service and booking fees goes unchallenged. These are not subject to any review, rule, or regulation. After pocketing the determined service charge and booking-fee amounts, it is now set to calculate its commission on the remaining of amount of the rider's fare. Through this scheme, Uber has been able to inflate its total take rate of the rider's fare to 55 percent and above, leaving 45 percent or less for the driver to cover all his cost burden and wages.

What makes it pathetic and unconscionable is the fact that as gas prices have soared, Uber has taken joy and delight in paying drivers less for any given trip, paying fifty-five to sixty-five cents per mile to cover all the costs, such as insurance, car notes, maintenance, and wages. They must be operating on a different planet or on the altar of sheer joyful exploitation because they can. The rideshare companies supply the platform for taxi services, which is a part of their regular business operations. Through connections and financial influence, Uber has fought indefatigably to thwart any legal framework that would give drivers reasonable earnings and some sort of protection against abuse and exploitation to satisfy its unsavory appetite for money.

One of the reasons is to ensure that drivers on the platform remain perpetual slave-laborers to be ruthlessly exploited for corporate wealth creation. From there, it has applied different techniques of psychological manipulation in many areas of its operation to exploit and condition drivers to its slave-labor policies. Usually, psychological manipulation begins with minor boundary violations that gradually escalate. This is evident in Uber's gradual increase in its total take rate from 25 to 33 to 48 to more than 60 percent now in some cases, without attempts from any regulatory agency to curb its predatory behavior. Total take rate here includes booking fee, service fee, and commission.

The second aspect of this psychological manipulation involves offering the lowest pay for a trip, thereby forcing drivers not astute enough to know the difference into accepting trips that are not worth their effort, out of frustration and despair. The company decides how many hours a driver can work, how much he earns per trip, when he has to sign off, and the pay date of his earnings, then turns around to disingenuously classify drivers as independent contractors without the benefit of taxi independent contractor gate fees.

A driver shoulders the cost of insurance, maintenance, gas, and car notes, and Uber decides what payment he is entitled to per trip based on its manipulation of booking and service fees. Then the company determines its take rate, all controlled and tallied subjectively. Rather than make sure drivers makes a fair, decent, livable wage, the rideshare companies will spend millions of dollars to wage all kinds of psychological and political warfare against the implementation of their rights, based on the conviction that a driver is unable to escape the situation and therefore bound to accept any unfair conditions to survive.

For part-time drivers trying to augment their income, the level of financial exploitation can be minimized. For professional drivers whose livelihoods depend on the digital taxi business, it's unrealistic to believe that their lot will ever get better, everything considered. It's an uphill task now for Uber and other rideshare professional drivers to sponsor their children through schools, pay their mortgages, and live the American dream.

Uber has spent millions of dollars in lobbying, campaign contributions, and other tactics to fight against regulatory enforcement in order to run an open slave-labor market with absolute authority and control over its drivers as slaves. With no regulations, no established standard of earning rate per mile, Uber is the one and only, with the power to determine the worth of drivers' labor without consideration of other economic variables affecting the transportation market.

This is nothing but absolute exploitation of labor—a concept defined as "one agent taking unfair advantage of another," which renowned economists, such as Adam Smith, refers to as an *optional moral injustice.* Whatever financial success the rideshare companies boast of, the drivers are the bridge-builders, or if you like, the powerhouse, and they deserve good financial returns on their investment. It's morally wrong and unjust for rideshare companies to treat these drivers as pawns in order to build financial empires through deceptive, exploitative policies that cheat drivers of their rights and fair share of earnings for the many hours of hard work they put in every day, using a deceptive platform that repays many hours of hard work with slave wages.

What happens, for example, if a trip is flashed on drivers' smartphones from morning till dawn and no driver picks it up? The rider can roll his smartphone up and down from morning till dawn and won't get picked up. In this regard, what keeps digital platforms alive financially are drivers, not the mere existence of the platforms.

Every time a driver accepts a pickup, he is taking a risk, the cost of which may not be quantified. Instead of recognizing these risks, Uber would rather resort to threats, such as temporary suspension of the driver from its platform for rejecting a certain number of trips, or deactivating the driver completely from the platform unless he stops in the middle of the road or freeway to take a photo of himself on its app. In the process of trying to exit to a location where he can take a photo of himself, who knows what he will encounter?

The Rider

Undoubtedly, riders are the core market force from which rideshare companies and drivers derive financial benefits. Naturally, riders save a little money riding on rideshare platforms. The discounts riders get, along with commission manipulations, come at the expense of drivers earning far below the minimum wage. Rideshare drivers are completely under the yoke of rideshare companies, subject to all kinds of manipulations and ruthless exploitation for profit maximization.

There is also a scheme in which riders are charged unusually high fares, called *surge periods*. These are periods of excessive demand or scarce supply of drivers. It is said that surge pricing uses microeconomics to calculate a market price for riders and drivers alike. But the scheme of surge pricing is simply a means of extorting money from both riders and drivers to widen the corporate profit margin. Believe it or not, it's nothing more than price-gouging.

Parallel taxi transport owners and operators never have the rights or permission to do surge pricing, such as when there are conventions or other events with hundreds or thousands of people coming into city, whether demand exceeds supply or not. Cities' transport systems usually put in place an established numerical link code—call it code3—to notify taxi companies, who will then link drivers to the event locations of excessive demand without additional cost to riders. It works very effectively.

The second situation happens locally. Most riders who live

in or close to the suburbs, or even in the city, have experienced a price surge whenever it serves the rideshare company's purpose of profiting more. What creates this situation is simple. Uber, for example, is stuck with its fifty-five cents per mile without taking into account the distance a driver has to drive to the pickup location, even as gas prices and maintenance costs have soared. While fares have skyrocketed on the digital rideshare market, driver pay per mile has been considerably slashed.

In essence, ridesharing companies have the luxury of taking undue advantage of real and imaginary situations in surge pricing to exploit both riders and drivers to feed their unsavory appetite for money.

Rideshare Drivers

The options available to drivers wanting to work on rideshare platforms such as Uber are to lease from an Uber-affiliated car rental company, such as Avis, or register their personal car on the platform.

Leasing to Drive for Uber

Uber and Uber-affiliated car-rental leasing policies require a seven-day rental agreement; otherwise, the right to rent and work on the platform is denied. It appears this policy contravenes independent contractors' rights to schedule working days unconditionally. The alternative is to rent from independent owners or other rental facilities, such as HYRE.

Uber and Avis rental-company policies make it difficult or impossible to get a refund in the middle of a seven-day period, no matter the circumstances. This simply precludes uncontrollable situations, such as health reasons and other emergency situations that may warrant a partial refund. With Uber and affiliated rental policies, that refund amount is gone forever.

Even regular cab companies would, for daily drivers, have the decency to give a Sunday free day, though drivers are rightly classified as independent contractors. In the olden days of slavery, slaves were forced to work ten or more hours a day, six days a week, with only the Sabbath off. Only house slaves worked seven days a week. How these policies align with independent-contractor freedom status is questionable. How are these policies different from those of the era of slavery, which offered no choice to the exploited laborer? They seem designed to pour an avalanche of abuse and exploitation, and consequently reintroduce the old master-slave practices of past centuries in the name of innovative transport technology—or should we call it innovative technology for enslaving drivers?

Using Your Car to Drive for Uber and Other Rideshare Companies

Using your car to drive in this business gives you the flexibility to choose the day, time, and drive. But that's not as rosy as it appears on the surface. What matters is the take-home wages after all expenses.

Often Uber and Lyft will put out advertisements promising exaggerated earnings of thousands of dollars per week or $26 per hour on weekends. This is nothing but a comical gimmick to entice drivers—and for public consumption. It sounds good and irresistible, but how much is the pay rate per mile on weekends? How many hours of driving will it take to earn this fat projected income? When car notes, insurance, gas, repairs and maintenance, depreciation, and number of hours worked are factored in, a consistent result of far below minimum wage is always arrived at.

Many empirical-data earning compilations have shown beyond a reasonable doubt that rideshare drivers earn less than minimum wage per hour. In addition, consider the undeniable fact that by subjecting a vehicle to so many miles of driving on a daily basis, there is a high probability of constant breakdowns involving costly repairs. One must have a car with the horsepower of a super-duty truck to withstand the engine stress and strain that ordinary cars are incapable of. In either case, whether leasing or using a personal car, rideshare drivers are the economic institution of digital taxi companies just as slaves were the economic institution of slave owners.

Uber has the hidden secret of starting its operation with a promised total take rate (total commission) of 25 percent of the rider's fare just to attract drivers. Once it attracts enough drivers, the total commission increases progressively to 33, 40, 48, 50, 60-plus percent with time. This is possible because Uber holds itself unaccountable for unfair practices and wrongful actions, which is why it will fight tooth and nail to derail any attempt by those in authority to enforce compliance within its commission continuum.

It is possible that, with time and in the absence of a legal framework of protection for drivers against exploitation and abuse, Uber's total commission will peak at 75 percent or more of the riders' pay, while drivers earnings plunge to 25 percent or less. As a matter of fact, Uber in some instances *has* kept more than 75 percent of a rider's fare.

An article in *Jalopnik*[7] cited a case of a rider paid $65 for a half-hour trip while the driver made only $15. Uber kept more than 75 percent of the fare, more than triple the average take rate it claims in financial reports with the Securities and Exchange Commission.

Also, an aricle in Full Stack Economics, Technology, and Public Policy (7b) cited a case a rider paid $59 for a six-mile trip to Arlington, Virginia. After a drop off, the driver received a base fare of of $16.52. Lyft pocketed $42.48, almost 75 percent of the fare just for dispatching a trip. The two examples, among many, many others, show the exploitation of riders and drivers without doubt. I could not help but wonder why airline fares are relatively cheaper.

---

[7] Dhruv Mehrotra and Aaron Gordon, "Uber And Lyft Take a Lot More from Drivers Than They Say," *Jalopnik* (August 26, 2019), https://jalopnik.com/uber-and-lyft-take-a-lot-more-from-drivers-than-they-sa-1837450373.

(7b). Timothy B. Lee: Idrove for Lyft for a week and learned its business model is broken.

Full Stack Economics

December 22, 2022.

www.fullstackeconomics.com

These statistical data—the amount Uber charged a rider against the pay a driver received—will be juxtaposed to give the reader a better picture of how drivers are the chattel of digital taxi platforms and clearly fit within the framework of what the renowned economist Adam Smith refers to as an *optional moral injustice.*

Operating an unregulated platform with no accountability and no transparency is gradually taking us back to the days of slavery and creating market environments of 21st-century jungle justice, in which drivers on rideshare platforms deserve to eat only the breadcrumbs dropping from the master's table. Through lies and unethical manipulations, drivers are seen and treated as the wretched of the earth, with all amount of disrespect and indignity, worse than roadside workers. Roadside workers have the power and choice to bargain for their labor cost.

Here are some of the statistics for analysis: For a trip from George Bush Intercontinental Airport in Houston, Texas, to deep inside Sugarland, a distance of 45 miles, Uber charged the rider $70.72, paid a base rate of $29.47, and added a paltry fifty-five cents fuel surcharge, equivalent of a 16.9-fluid-ounce water bottle of gas, bringing the total paid to the driver to $30.02. Going by Uber's algorithm for calculating its commission, let's assume for simplicity a maximum booking fee of $10 and a service fee of $8, totaling $18. $70.72 − 18.00 = $52.72, and 25 percent commission on $52.72 equals $13.18. Uber's total commission would be $18.00 + $13.18 = $31.18, meaning the driver should have earned $39.54. Adding a fuel surcharge of

George Inuen

$0.55 would bring the driver's total earning to $39.99. Right here, the driver has lost $9.97, on the assumption of the maximum allowable booking fee and service fee. Otherwise, he would have earned far above $39.99.

The point highlighted here is the unfair manipulation and dishonesty in milking as much money as possible from drivers in any way they can. The fare from Bush airport to the lower end of Kingwood or upper end of Greenspoint area is about $29.47. Even a shuttle bus carrying fifteen or more passengers would not take a customer from Bush airport to deep inside Sugarland for $29.47.

Some additional examples:

- For a trip from Bellaire, Houston, Texas, to Bush airport, Uber charged the customer $39.78, paid the driver a base rate of $18.55, added a $0.55 fuel surcharge to bring the total to $19.10, and pocketed $20.68 profit.
- For a trip from Bush airport to a dropoff location 42.3 miles away, Uber charged the customer $53.00, paid the driver $27.77, and pocketed $25.23 profit.
- For a trip of about 14 miles, Uber charged the customer $20.00, paid the driver $9.79, and pocketed $10.21 profit.
- For a trip of about 10.5 miles, Uber charged the customer $17.00, paid the driver $7.92, and pocketed $9.08 profit.

- For a trip of 24.8 miles from Harris County, Houston, to 28000 Southwest Freeway, Rosenberg, Uber charged the customer $30.00, paid the driver a total of $14.94, and pocketed $15.06, equal to 50.2 percent.

- For a trip from Brookhollow, west loop south, to Bush airport, Uber charged the customer $40.00, paid the driver a recalculated fee of $15.90, and pocketed $24.10 profit.

- For a trip from Bush airport to 1100 Texas Avenue in downtown Houston, Uber charged the customer $35.00, paid the driver a paltry $12.86, and pocketed $22.14 profit.

For the above sampling, Uber collected a total of $305.50 from the eight customers, paid the driver $141.82, and pocketed $168.68 of the total, which translates to 55.21 percent commission (take rate) for dispatching eight trips, while the driver earned $168.68 or 44.79 percent of the total to cover gas, his car note, insurance, car depreciation, maintenance, and wages.

For these eight trips, the driver's earning averaged $17.73 per trip. When distance, gas, insurance, car note, and maintenance costs are factored in, the driver's actual earning is far below the minimum wage. I am not yet sure if oil companies' margin of profitability per barrel of oil or other refined petroleum products sold is as high as what Uber makes per trip dispatched.

The examples go on and on, but the sample of data given above and subsequent data from research groups will certainly shed some light on how drivers are victims of financial exploitation for unfathomable wealth creation in billions of dollars for digital taxi platforms through slave wages to ensure discounted transportation platforms remain affordable and sustainable at the expense of drivers. Also, the above statistical data will give a rider some idea of why drivers reject and/or cancel trips, resulting in a very long waiting time or no-show.

Uber increased rider fares considerably after the pandemic, while at the same time greatly slashing drivers' earnings for the same trip distance. Uber and other rideshare platforms couldn't care less about the skyrocketing prices of every conceivable product. Right here one can see that Uber's secret agenda of exploitation and abuse of drivers is consistent with what the renowned economist Adam Smith refers to as an *optional moral injustice*. It is an ostentatious display of the company's hidden agenda to ruthlessly use drivers as chattel, a commodity in trade.

Some years ago, Uber paid $20 million to settle a Federal Trade Commission (FTC) complaint that it had systematically deceived drivers about their potential earnings and the terms of a lease deal it offered to help them acquire cars. The company got away without admitting or denying the charges, but the details offered by the FTC paint a picture of a company engaged in wholesale deception in order to recruit drivers.

Believe it or not, the $20 million fine Uber paid inflicted no financial pain. Uber has all the power on earth to raise $20 million in a few hours by slashing drivers' earnings and manipulating its total commission rate to pay the fine. It is answerable to nobody and not accountable to any authority for violating, cheating, and deceiving drivers completely under its yoke. Fining the company without mandating rules and regulations to protect drivers from unlimited assault and exploitation serves little to no purpose. They will always get back to their psychological tricks of exploitation and abuse, knowing they can always hold drivers to ransom, chipping away at drivers' earnings to bail themselves out of any fines for deceitful and unethical business practices.

It's not like the FTC, other regulatory agencies, lawmakers, or the secretary of Federal transportation are not aware of this 21st-century platform of exploitation. They just lack the courage and the fortitude to call a spade a spade. When an entity constantly shows a propensity to dishonesty, lying, and cheating, and nothing is done to curb it, it certainly amounts to empowering that entity to continue its deceitful practices. The ability of rideshare companies to balloon their commission from 25 percent to almost 60 percent is proof positive of this.

This unprecedented exploitation, abuse, and denial of the gate-fee rights of these drivers without a call to order from any regulatory commission or agency has put drivers on the receiving end of the deal in the digital-taxi marketplace. The drivers, not Uber, are the actual sponsors and legitimate vessels of this low-cost platform, being the ones who accept ruthlessly discounted earnings and are exploited with impunity.

Digital taxi companies have demonstrated a willingness to engage in a persistent scheme of fraudulent extortion of money from drivers, echoed in statements such as, "We pay because we can"—a stark reminder of the power and arrogance of slave-masters over their slaves. Many research findings have been published on rideshare companies' secret agenda to exploit drivers to create unlimited corporate wealth for themselves and their cronies.

A research article published by *Mission Local*[8] offers a snapshot of how rideshare drivers are scammed of their fair share of the rider's payment and gives further insight into how drivers have become their chattel. I'll add some comments along the way:

As rideshare prices skyrocket, Uber and Lyft take a bigger piece of riders' payments

We booked 10 rides with Uber and 10 with Lyft. Drivers pocketed an average of 52 percent of our fares
by David Mamaril Horowitz

On a July weekday afternoon, I booked an Uber to my Visitacion Valley home, a 2.5 mile trip for $17.16. My driver—we'll call him Ryan— showed me how much he made: $7.54.

So $17.16 – $7.54 = $9.62 is what Uber pocketed.

Uber has long claimed that the amount it takes from fares on average, known as a "take rate,"

[8] . David Mamaril Horowitz, "As Rideshare Prices Skyrocket, Uber and Lyft Take a Bigger Piece of Riders' Payments," *Mission Local* (July 15, 2021), https://missionlocal.org/2021/07/as-rideshare-prices-skyrocket-uber-and-lyft-take-a-bigger-bite-of-the-pie/.

is around 25 percent, yet the driver got just 44 percent of my payment. A cursory Google search can quickly pull up screenshots that show this is nothing new, and many media outlets have collected data shedding insight on the companies' take rates.

What's new is the growing appetite of the rideshare companies. Not satisfied with 25 percent, they now appear to need or want more—frequently half of the fare and, in some cases, nearly three times the publicized take rate, according to the bottom line on 20 recent rides.

Perhaps the most exhaustive attempt to track rideshare companies' take rate was in 2019, when the media outlet Jalopnik examined 14,756 fares and concluded that Uber kept 35 percent of the revenue, while Lyft kept 38 percent. (Uber and Lyft disputed these analyses but did not provide data sets to Jalopnik upon request showing otherwise.)

Even when they charge the customer more or when demand is higher and the prices are higher, the driver does not benefit from the price hike, even five cents!

Mission Local decided it was time to again track the companies' take rates. We booked 20 rides in San Francisco with drivers who shared their pay for our trips. Drivers said demand is indeed back up and prices are higher, but none said they noticed more pay per trip.

The unscientific sampling showed that, of 10 rides, drivers with Uber received an average of 56 percent of what I paid; of 10 with Lyft, drivers received an average of 47 percent of what I paid. Of all 20, drivers took home an average of 52 percent of what I got charged.

Uber's new algorithm that allows drivers to see trip earnings and destinations before accepting a trip is nothing but a fraud as long as the projected drivers' earnings are not related in any way to its commission as a function of the rider's fare. The amount a passenger pays and the amount a driver is paid for any trip are not at all related. It's a pure black-market trading place.

The new algorithm allows Uber to pay a driver $12.86 for a trip of twenty-four miles. It charges the rider $34.00 and pockets $21.14 profit just for dispatching a trip. A trip of this distance will consume about one to one and one tenth of a gallon of gas. Assuming the cost of one gallon of gas is $4, and add other miscellaneous expenses at a conservative estimate of $2, the approximate amount the driver earned for the trip is $5.00 or $6.86. A regular taxi fare for the same-distance trip is about $56.00. Comparing the amount earned for dispatching a trip against what is paid to a driver, there can be no doubt in anybody's mind of the inhumane and unconscionable exploitation of those in dire poverty struggling to keep their heads above water.

From an economic perspective, digital taxi platforms act as quasi-governments in the sense that nobody regulates them. This enables them to milk billions of dollars out of these drivers to invest in other sectors of the economy, with the assurance that if and when the racket collapses, they can go elsewhere.

That aside, it would be interesting and worth noting for economists, financial experts, and people of all walks of life to embrace an economic model that pays on the average sixty-five cents a mile, for which the operator shoulders all the financial costs—car note, insurance, gas, repair and maintenance, depreciation, and wages—as a model of economic prosperity and upward mobility. And if so embraced, why was the colonial platform of exploitation and slavery or the trading policies of merchants of medieval times ever rejected? The philosophy and psychology in the scheme of exploitation is rooted in the belief that most drivers are under the threat of poverty, coupled with drivers being stereotyped as imbeciles and ignorant.

It's not so. It's the opportunity of being at the right place at the right time with the tools necessary for advancement. I know for sure that many are equipped with the tools but never have the opportunity. It's inhumane and unconscionable exploitation to charge a rider $40.00 and pay a driver $15.90.

Some countries have realized that the rideshare platform model of discounted fares, with all its bluster, is designed to exploit poorer citizens who happen to be Uber or other rideshare drivers to impoverishment. These countries have taken a realistic approach to correct the imbalance in income distribution. Models like this should touch the conscience of people of all walks of life.

Uber has suspended services in Tanzania due to a pricing order proposed by the Land Transport Regulatory Authority (LATRA), saying in a statement on Thursday, April 14, 2022, that the country has made it challenging for platforms like Uber to continue to operate. Under the new regulations, fares doubled to 900 Tanzania shillings (0.4, 0.3 euros) per kilometer. Meanwhile, maximum commission for rideshare companies was set at 15 percent, down from the previous 33 percent.

The transport regulator said the changes were aimed at maintaining competition and ensuring affordable taxis, saying all providers save for Uber had conformed to the new regulations. Uber said it would not be able to provide services until the environment became friendlier. When does the environment become friendly? one may ask. Uber launched in Tanzania in 2016 starting with a take rate of 25 percent, after which it went up to 33 percent. As long as Uber is allowed to increase its commission to any level, pay citizens who happen to drive for Uber any slave wages unhindered, that has to be a friendly environment in which to operate.

To set price regulation limits on how a rider's fare will be split between the company and the drivers creates a hostile environment that is unacceptable to Uber. On the other hand, allowing Uber to impose its will on regulators, take control of the country's ground transportation system, deploy all kinds of unfair tactics to avoid regulatory enforcement, and pay the citizens who drive for Uber slave wages for any trip, and you have created a friendly environment for Uber. Create a space for Uber, allow it to exploit and abuse your citizens as slaves—that's a friendly environment that warrants a friendly handshake between regulators and Uber.

Maybe I'm wrong. Let's consider some other factors that can fetter the operation of Uber in Tanzania and other countries opposed to its exploitative wages and lack of transparency.

Does Uber fervently wish to introduce a system of increased productivity but is held back by regulations from its mission of a new gospel of economic world order of prosperity? *Increased productivity* refers to more goods and services that increase people's standard of living. Is a rideshare platform a key driver of economic growth of countries, regions, and cities? In short, can a rideshare platform improve the economy of countries in which it operates by creating meaningful high-paying jobs? What about the GDP growth of a country in which it operates?

In comparison to technologies that have changed the world, such as the Internet, artificial intelligence, telephones, television, and so on, how really has the Uber rideshare platform benefited mankind? Examining the lack of transparency and forthrightness in their operations, the unlimited power to extort money from drivers and riders, there is not a shred of doubt that rideshare drivers are the financial institution that rideshare companies exploit to propel themselves into other business ventures, or salvage themselves from financial woes and failures in those ventures. In fact, rideshare companies use drivers as their springboard and a tool for wealth creation, having the unilateral power to slash their earnings in whatever manner and methods they deem necessary to raise funds for their financial ventures, satisfy their corporate greed, and above all maintain drivers as an inexhaustible source of revenue-generation.

Maybe now that Tanzania has set the tone for a fair share between digital taxi operators and drivers, other reluctant, hesitant regulators and lawmakers influenced by campaign contributions and other forms of legalized bribery will be courageous enough to set standards that serve the interest of all parties involved. Riders should also understand the physical stress, financial costs, and sacrifice drivers undertake to provide the service they need, only to be rewarded with slave wages. Some of them don't even show courtesy, not to talk of giving tips as appreciation.

The fact of the matter is, the goal of Uber and other rideshare companies is to create a free global market environment void of any type of regulatory enforcement that guarantees protection for drivers, thereby giving them all the power to exploit, enslave, and abuse drivers fiendishly to satisfy their unsavory appetite for money. All one has to do is listen to the evasive, ludicrous defense that officials of the rideshare companies make when confronted with their lack of transparency and the slave wages paid drivers as they pocket almost 60 percent of the fare just for dispatching a trip.

"We don't force people to drive for us" and "We pay because we can" are the answers these officials give whenever complaints are made by drivers and non-driver groups about the unfair and unreasonable low pay drivers receive for their services. What do you, as a fair- minded person, think of statements or utterances like this from the highest echelon of a business establishment you affiliate with or partner with? Insensitive, awful, arrogant, or an open declaration of horrendous abuse of power with the assurance that they are shielded and protected, so what can you do to us?

Is it the fact that drivers—often retirees, immigrants, and people of color—are not financially important to lawmakers of the different political parties, have nobody to fight for their rights, and are no match for rideshare taxi companies in terms of financial capability that has warranted this unprecedented exploitation and abuse? If ever, and whenever, the truth about all the manipulations, lies, and price-fixing shall be exposed, it certainly will be mind-boggling.

All the relevant authorities and agencies must put their heads together to arrive at a solution that is fair and beneficial to all parties involved. One of the core issues in Uber's unethical practice has been deceit and lack of transparency and forthrightness in its operations. After starting operation with a false promise of a 25 percent commission, it would, as years of its operation progressed, spend millions of dollars to obstruct any legal framework of protection for the drivers, thereby giving itself the unilateral power to exploit drivers at will, treating them like the slaves of past centuries.

Why It Matters

Uber has undertaken an extraordinary experiment in behavioral science to subtly entice an independent workforce to maximize its growth. It has also devised all kinds of psychological tricks aimed at having complete control of its drivers to maximize profits. While Uber is focused mainly on how to manipulate, control, and exploit its drivers at will, it is also creating situations in which these drivers are vulnerable to psychological risk factors, such as anxiety disorder and depression, distraction, and lack of concentration while transporting a rider. This is not concerning to rideshare taxi companies, since the financial responsibilities vis-à-vis insurance claims and damages to a driver's car are craftily avoided.

The probability of a rider riding in a distraught Uber driver's car is always there, and the consequences can be costly. This, of course, can be a byproduct of the realization, among other factors, that all the money one invested in the rideshare business went to create unfathomable wealth for rideshare companies while you are steadily being driven into an abyss of unrecoverable poverty.

Sounds like a fairy tale? Wait till major repairs, such as engine and transmission problems, along with the car notes, insurance, gas, maintenance, depreciation, and probably accident insurance claims surface like a monster, resulting in bankruptcy. At that point, the truth of being the chattel of rideshare platforms will be quite evident, the false promise of economic prosperity and upward mobility completely shattered, and the fact of being a slave-laborer obvious. This can never be and will never be the path to meaningful job creation and economic prosperity, when a driver gets paid fifteen dollars for a trip Uber charged a rider sixty-five dollars for.

The false advertisement of a driver earning $26 an hour driving weekends or earning $1,800 or more a week has to be the height of lies, deceit, and comical gimmicks full of hypocritical tendencies. For one thing, Uber, with this blustering claim, has never stated different weekend rates for drivers, such as $1.20 per mile, as a justification. Unfortunately, Uber, Lyft, and other rideshare companies are exploiting drivers to impoverishment by aggressively fighting against legislative proposals and regulatory enforcement that will guarantee a meaningful and decent earning rate per mile for drivers. They always fight in the ways they know best. Such proposals are dead in the womb and never see the light of the day.

Drivers fight to free themselves from slave wages, while rideshare companies fight to keep them in perpetual slavery and servitude. When Uber for all intents and purposes pays a driver fifty-five to sixty-five cents per mile because it can, is that not taking undue advantage to exploit and enslave these drivers, whose expenses continue to rise? If you think not, we must be living in two different worlds.

To gain a better perspective on the predicament rideshare drivers face, consider an employee of an establishment who uses his car for the service of the establishment, such as delivery. In most cases, he earns nothing for first twenty-five miles, counted as the distance from home to work. Thereafter, the driver starts earning forty-four cents or more per mile, in addition to salary and benefits. That employee's total pay package is the regular salary plus mileage earnings in compensation for using his car. In addition, the driver is entitled to all the benefits the establishment offers to its employees.

Now consider the predicament and absolute abuse and exploitation of a rideshare driver. He earns on the average sixty-five cents per mile, which must cover his car note, gas, insurance, maintenance, depreciation, and wages. The Uber driver gets no benefits, no salary, no medical coverage, only the sixty-five cents per mile. He has no other type of coverage to provide a safety net for a rainy day. The rideshare pay structure offers no economic prosperity, only economic suicide for drivers by impoverishing them miserably. The driver will find it impossible to replace his old car when there is a need, and in case of emergencies, there is nothing to fall back on by way of savings to meet medical expenses for himself or family members.

Uber's proclamation that it is "nothing more than a neutral technological platform, designed simply to enable drivers and passengers to transact the business of transportation" is far from the truth. In fact, Uber uses its platform to collect a fare from a rider, and what the driver receives is not related to what a passenger paid. Knowing that these drivers are desperate to make a living, Uber offers the lowest pay possible for a trip, lower than even shuttle buses would accept, assured that out of the many drivers out there, some will accept the low pay it offers out of despair and frustration. This is one of the psychological schemes Uber has employed to frustrate a driver into accepting whatever it offers as pay for a given trip. The difference is that it is not using the whip that slave masters used but converting lack of enforceable regulatory control and lack of accountability into a whip.

This is particularly true of long-distance trips, for which Uber charges the rider a high fare while in turn offering the lowest pay possible to a driver to maximize profit. To accomplish this, it has a habit of putting drivers in abeyance, with a message of "trip request paused," if they reject a certain number of trips— all in an effort to coerce drivers into accepting trips that are not worth their while.

It doesn't end there. If drivers continue rejecting consecutive trips that pay nothing but slave wages, they are completely deactivated from the system unless they stop in the middle of the road or freeway to take a selfie on the app before they can be signed in to take trips again. The rationale behind this is to force drivers to make a decision as to whether they want to accept a trip or not. Now, when drivers make a decision not to accept trips that they consider not worth their while, they are penalized.

This is in contradiction of a policy of allowing a driver to make a decision as whether to accept a trip or not. The real motive behind this psychological technique is simple: offer the lowest earning amount for a given trip and wait for the lowest bidder. The objective is to ruthlessly slash the driver's earnings and leave him with no choice but to accept or reject whatever it offers as his earning for any trip. This is true because Uber knows that once a driver has signed in on the platform, he needs to make a living and is therefore compelled to accept.

All these psychological tactics of coercion are comparable to abusers who use unethical tactics to coerce their victims into submission or silence. There are no tactics too unethical, no pressure too inhumane, that Uber and other rideshare companies would not employ to force drivers to dance to their music in order to exploit and abuse them. A driver is obligated to drive three or more miles to pick up a trip of twenty-four miles and get paid eleven dollars—a trip for which Uber charges the rider thirty-four dollars or more.

Gas tanks are not filled with free air. There is no rideshare company market with free tires and free repairs, and no supplemental benefits to augment all the financial and labor costs and hardship a driver incurs. Of course, why would there be? These companies have classified drivers as independent contractors, refused to treat them as employees in order to deny them any benefits entitlement, and took away their power to unionize so they can't fight for their rights. This is tantamount to slavery and a gross violation of human rights.

The irate statements of executives of digital taxi platforms when confronted about slave wages paid to drivers show how intolerant they are of proposals aimed at putting just a little more money in the pockets of drivers in order to improve their living standards. What a dubious if not a devious platform, lacking in compassion for today's economic realities. Rideshare taxi companies do not provide a discount to offset any type of costs drivers incur. The only reward drivers get is dehumanization and a gross violation of their human rights. This has to be the greatest exploitative slave-labor trading and marketing platform ever assembled.

We need to stop boxing shadows and call a rideshare taxi platform that strips drivers of their independent-contractor-status rights, does not accord them the status of employees, has the unilateral power to decide what amount they can earn for any given trip, offers no type of medical benefits, employs psychological tactics to dehumanize them, robs them of any right to fare negotiation, schedules when to sign off, and schedules when they get paid (unless instant payment request is requested) what it is, without mincing words: a platform of exploitation and slavery.

It was this type of exploitation and abuse that brought about the enactment of all kinds of protection laws, but when certain entities can operate in any manner they want, then they are not simply above regulations but empowered to recreate a platform for the master-slave relationship of past centuries. Those who lived through it, if still alive, never forget, and those still going through it will always remember.

Now that Uber, Lyft, and a coalition of large corporations are expanding their quest to rope off workers from labor laws, we must not forget how it was in past centuries: the creation of abject poverty, chaos, and violence that resulted in wanton destruction of lives and property. Those companies and some legislators want to introduce new legislation, the Worker Flexibility and Choice Act, that wouldn't just help Uber and Lyft and other rideshare companies treat their drivers as independent contractors but exempt virtually any American worker from minimum wage and overtime protections. We must give serious thought as to whether we want to go back to the colonial days of slavery and the way things were before, or move forward with the American ideals where anybody who works hard can live the American dream.

The proposed legislation, if passed, would probably show that we cannot transcend the colonial slavery platform of the past. We are gradually moving closer and closer to the final stage of creating an elephant in the room. Those who do not remember the past are condemned to repeat it.

Nobody, whether by virtue of connections, campaign contributions, or what have you, should entertain any illusions as to what this proposed bill, if enacted into law, will lead our society to: the dark days of slavery, gun violence, poverty, and insecurity. Is this the new society we want to create in the 21st century, or do we want to move forward to create a society where every talented person is guaranteed the American dream without any dose of infringement on their God-given talents whatsoever?

Whether this proposed legislation is designed to take us back to the colonial days or create a prosperous and peaceful society for all Americans irrespective of color and creed remains to be seen, but make no mistake: if and when the exploited are fed up, things may get out of control. Unfortunately, the FTC and other regulatory agencies charged with the responsibility of preserving the conditions of free and fair markets have done nothing to protect drivers and workers alike from this type of assault and abuse.

Cases in which many people have quit their jobs and taken out loans to buy cars—Ube-x, Uber-pro, and so on—as an investment venture on the Uber platform, hoping to own an asset; piled up debts they can't service; or ended up homeless and suicidal because of poor earnings are numerous to list. A Google search can help get more facts.

An NBC News report[9] reveals that in Kenya, drivers say Uber has ruined their lives. A Kenyan who quit his job to drive for Uber thought he had made it. He was able to rent a good apartment, borrowed money for a down payment on a compact car, and took a loan from a microfinance and loan company. Years later, Uber slashed its fares and the driver's income. Unable to cope with mounting debts, he fell behind on his rent, and the driver and his family were evicted from their apartment in Nairobi. Car maintenance is costly, fuel prices are high, insurance is high, and instead of owning an asset, he is now saddled with growing debt.

The report quotes the driver as saying, "When you have a family to feed, kids to pay school fees for, rents to pay, a loan to pay and your work is too much and exploitative, what happens?" It adds, "Interviews with more than 80 current and former drivers in Nairobi and the port city of Mombasa show that, in Kenya's biggest markets, untold numbers of Uber drivers are drowning in debt."

Drivers took out loans to purchase new vehicles with the false hope and promise that rideshare platforms would help them generate high income. Unfortunately, these drivers found themselves incapable of paying back their loans due to reduction

---

[9] . Amanda Sperber, "Uber Made Big Promises in Kenya. Drivers Say It's Ruined Their lives," NBC News (Nov. 29, 2020), https://www.nbcnews.com/news/world/uber-made-big-promises-kenya-drivers-say-it-s-ruined-n1247964.

of earnings, which adversely affected their income expectation. This is a good summary of how the Uber platform has driven drivers into abject poverty while Uber, with its deceptive promise of fantastic earnings, is making millions of dollars from the sweat of these struggling drivers.

The report continues: "But Uber drivers in Kenya are not alone in their experiences. … In December 2018, researchers from Washington University in St. Louis concluded that driving for UberX "increases hardship among the [low- and moderate-income] population, primarily by decreasing overall take-home pay." The same lies and deceit, the same techniques of financial exploitation of drivers is taking place here today.

What are the takeaways here? If nothing is done to protect the rights of drivers and workers alike, the gig-economy-platform model of exploitation will eventually be an acceptable institutionalized standard of practice. Applied to blue- or white-collar workers, this platform will not have stood the test of time. These have always followed and adhered to certain regulations and ethical framework standards that spread economic prosperity to the operators and workers. Anything outside economic prosperity for all participants is tantamount to economic moral injustice.

Uber's inherent culture of deception and exploitation is best summarized by Uber's payment of $20 million to settle an FTC complaint that it had systematically deceived drivers about their potential earnings and the terms of a lease deal it offered to help them acquire cars. The continuum of this culture of deception, ranging from extortion of money from drivers, extortion of money from riders in the name surge pricing, coercion, and unethical psychological tactics of subjugation, is still going on unabated today.

Basically, when a driver's phone goads him with the familiar chime of incoming trip offers, refusing them is like refusing money waved in your face. The natural reaction is a rush to accept the trip before trying to figure out if it's worth your while. One of the reasons this culture of lies and deception is flourishing today is because most drivers are so consumed with the idea of earning money that they have fallen victim to psychological tricks. Uber has carefully designed a program of around-the-clock opportunities to deprive them of the time to pause and think. Part of this thinking involves data collection relating to your earnings per trip against the amount the rider was charged for the same trip.

This is one way a driver can have a good insight into how he has been used and abused, while Uber is taking the credit and glory for creating a discounted transportation platform at the driver's expense. Sometimes, no matter the financial burden and pressure, one has to allow one's spirit to take leave of the physical being unhindered and wander in the realms of the spiritual world for a while in order to see the map of the forest more clearly. In doing so, the wisdom and economic benefit of earning twelve or thirteen dollars for a trip of twenty-four miles or more, for which Uber charged the rider thirty-five dollars or more, would be questioned and carefully examined.

For the same trip distance, a regular taxi driver earns fifty-six dollars or more. Uber has always maintained that lower rates are good for drivers, since it means increased utilization and higher earnings. In reality, it's like classroom theoretical concepts. In practice, environmental variable factors in conjunction with theoretical tools allow us to achieve the desired goals and objectives. What is the utilization rate at twelve dollars for the same-distance trip a taxi driver earns about fifty-six dollars for? How many twelve-dollar trips, how many miles behind the wheel, how much gas expense, labor cost, and other associated expenses will allow a driver to break even at fifty-five cents per mile?

In economics, business, and cost accounting, *break-even point* refers to the point at which total cost and total revenue are equal, meaning there is no loss or gain. Conventional wisdom dictates that this type of slave-labor pay structure offers take-home pay (wages) below minimum wage, with no prospect of prosperity, only poverty. Many research findings have confirmed that the rideshare pay structure actually impoverishes drivers.

There is no way to be better-off financially unless there are no bills, such as rent, utility, car notes, and insurance. The undisputable truth is that rideshare drivers are the chattel of rideshare companies for immense wealth creation, while being impoverished miserably. The truth really stares a driver in the face when problems like engine or transmission repair or replacement of car parts depletes his small savings, if he has any at all. The vehicle is worthless, and the funds to buy another from any savings made while driving for the rideshare company are at zero.

Earning twelve or thirteen dollars for a trip of this distance is simply paying for your gas, lunch, and a paltry earning of about five dollars, with a pat on the back saying "Thank you, boy." A trip of this distance, to and from, takes more than an hour and more than a gallon of gas, depending on the car type.

Most write-ups I have read, like a recent one from *Travel Off Path*,[10] focus on how Uber became affordable "because it was heavily subsidized by investors," and the financial loss it has suffered over "the five-odd years since the company's finances became public." It went on to talk about Uber fares going up, noting that "at the end consumers are the ones who are suffering: Uber fares are at a record high with no end in sight."

The role of investors can be applied in several ways, but the main responsibility is to commit funding for a program or project. There are economic factors affecting fares going up, but the drivers, whether they are included as the end-consumers or not, are the ones really suffering because they do not benefit from fares going up but rather have their earnings fiendishly slashed due to a dishonest, manipulative pay structure inherent to the company's algorithms.

This abuse and exploitation of drivers matters and should be a concern to all who fought hard to end exploitation and slavery, especially when listening to utterances like "We do not force people to drive for us." When drivers and other people of good will complain about the slave wages offered to a driver for a trip,

---

[10] Marvin Scholz, "Your Next Uber Is Going to Cost You a Lot More," *Travel Off Path* (May 29, 2022), https://www.traveloffpath.com/your-next-uber-is-going-to-cost-you-a-lot-more/.

you get an answer such as, "We pay because we can," which is tantamount to an admission of guilt.

If these types of statements reflect company policy, then it is a policy of consummate callousness and lack of empathy toward drivers. I am convinced that the world, in particular people who have respect for human dignity, their societal class notwithstanding, despise these types of egocentric attitudes and statements. If statements like this are a show of obsession for exploitation, a declaration to the world that they have successfully rolled the clock back to the days of slavery, or just for pure sensationalism, one thing is obvious: the more power these companies have to operate unregulated and unchecked, the more callous their inclination to treat drivers as slaves will become.

Utterances like these show the extent to which rideshare companies are willing to exploit, abuse, and cheat drivers to create wealth for themselves. There should be no doubt in anybody's mind about the abuse and the level of exploitation drivers endure on a daily basis because of their stereotyped status in the society. The words we say or statements we make, whether they project corporate or individual policy, reveal in no small dimension our character and who we are. They can either provoke contempt or inspire great thoughts and admiration.

The beginning of the first quarter of the 21st century, precisely the year 2008, "Yes We Can" became a household phrase in the US and globally. It assures all citizens that America's beacon still burns bright, and it will continue to burn bright if we do not go back to the ways things were before. "Yes We Can" envisions economic prosperity for all Americans irrespective of their social status, color, or creed. "Yes, We Can" called for a more perfect union, fairness, and forthrightness in our dealings with each other.

And now, at the beginning of the second quarter of the 21st century, comes a different type of "Yes We Can": We can exploit, abuse, cheat, and pay our drivers any amount of money we want, "Because We Can," by using our platforms to operate the ways things were done during the era of slavery. "Because We Can" envisions economic prosperity for a few who are willing to perpetuate economic injustice on those in dire need of survival by ruthlessly exploiting them and tearing their spirits down.

And so, we have two faces, two visions of "Yes We Can": one for the first quarter and another for the second quarter of the 21st century. A documentary series depicting these two philosophies of "Yes We Can" and "Because We Can" is in the making.

"Because We Can" fits in perfectly with the money, power, and connections that shield and exonerate rideshare companies from the guilt of horrendous abuse. This "Because We Can" is focused on creating a slave-labor market globally with absolute control of its drivers, paying slave wages without any penalty for violating regulatory laws and human rights. The evidence of this comes to light in its unrelenting efforts to pressure officials in many countries for some form of active noncompliance with regulations. Countries in which people of integrity and honesty refuse to sell their citizens to be exploited and enslaved are often declared to be creating an unfriendly environment.

It remains to be seen how much longer relevant agencies and society in general will remain complicit to a platform that inflicts blistering financial hardship on drivers through deception and lies, and extorts money from riders in the name of surge pricing to create immense wealth for itself. There is a saying that there is a limit to human endurance. To impoverish drivers this way, chipping away at their earnings, is not only distasteful but absolute slavery, and we need to call it what it is. It is not an understatement to say that the right to make a decent living as an independent-contractor driver based on gate fee is gradually slipping away, and the ability of the rideshare taxi companies to entrench themselves as the slave masters of rideshare drivers is on the rise in the absence of transparency, regulations, and accountability.

CHAPTER 4

Uber Eats

Uber Eats delivery consumes so much time and exposes the driver to great danger, yet the pay is so little that sometimes one cannot help but wonder if the reward is worth the risk. Perhaps the delivery drivers have never taken time to examine the pay they receive after each delivery. The act of driving some miles to pick up from restaurants, sometimes two restaurants, and deliver to two different locations that are not close to each other (double batch), can take forty-five minutes to over an hour.

A comparison of what Uber charges the customer to what Uber pays the delivery driver will surely leave you shaking your head. A double-batch delivery, requiring pickups from two restaurants and delivery to two different locations, one on the third floor of an office building and the other at a residence, was billed for $10.80. After completing the delivery, the driver was paid only $3.06. Uber pocketed $10.80 − $3.06 = $7.74, or 71.66 percent.

Delivery poses the risk of a driver being robbed, and the car being stolen or towed. The possibility of an attack by dogs

71

cannot be ruled out. How much more indignity can you subject a person to for a delivery trip of forty-five or more minutes for a paltry $3.06 while pocketing $7.38 just for taking the food-delivery order by a phone linked to a digital taxi platform?

CHAPTER 5

Signing On to Drive

The moment a driver signs up to start driving, he is allotted the number of hours he can operate for the day. Toward the end, the driver will be notified as to how many minutes he has left to operate. When the time comes, it's like a parent telling a child, "Time to go bed." At this point, the driver is completely deactivated from the system.

As independent contractors, do drivers really need to be told it's time to go home? They are adults and can decide when and when not to go home. It's their life. It's their business. It's their right to make their own decision. They do not really need to be told to close down.

The reason for this deactivation, says Uber, is for the health and safety of the drivers, so what about reasonable pay above minimum wage for the financial well-being of drivers, so they can go home on time? If indeed Uber cares for the well-being of drivers, why not accept them as employees, and if not, why fight against the long-established independent-contractor rights and benefits of the taxi business?

What's the motive behind not being transparent about what riders pay and the take rate as a function of a driver's earnings? How does a driver determine the worth of his trip versus what he earns for a trip? This appears to be a deliberate scheme designed to exploit a driver as much as possible, since the driver has no way to negotiate for a pay commensurate with the amount the rider is charged.

CHAPTER 6

Payment of Earnings

Superficially, this scam scheme may not attract much attention, but a little scrutiny shows how meticulously Uber uses drivers' earnings to generate additional revenue for itself. While Uber has a provision for instant-pay request, with a transfer fee above eighty-five cents, it usually schedules when a driver gets paid.

This is the interest a drivers pays for requesting his hard-earned money paid to his account ahead of Uber's schedule payment date.

Depending on the number of days of driving a week, Uber schedules payments in two batches. Usually, the first batch of payments takes five to six days, and the second payment almost the same length of time. So, while Uber is getting fatter and wealthier, the driver is gradually but steadily getting leaner and poorer.

You don't have to be a mathematician to figure this out. The business interest Uber earns through this scheme nationwide, worldwide, is astronomical. This, along with the scheme that robs drivers of their fair share of riders' fares, and extorting money from riders in the name of surge pricing, is the reason Uber will do anything, employ any tactics, to drown the drivers with stones around their necks. It's also one of the reasons Uber is able to spend millions of dollars to maintain and sustain this slave-labor market at all costs.

CHAPTER 7

Political Theatre

America has earned the appellation—God's own country. This appellation and honor is laden with expectation of a near perfect society and country where every right of the human being is guaranteed without a dose of overbearing infringement or discrimination whatsoever. The Christian Faith Trumpet, November 1, 2009

One of the problems in our country today is toxicity and divisiveness in the political arena. In retrospect, issues affecting struggling citizens and their welfare have been unduly politicized. The Yes on Proposition 22 campaign in California is a clear example.

Things are not done the way they were before because of technological advancement. Laws and regulations have to be amended to protect the rights and welfare of workers correspondingly. The rights of app-based drivers and gig workers have remained virtually unchanged. App-based drivers are denied the right to unionize, denied independent-contractor gate-fee rights, left unprotected, and sold out completely to rideshare digital taxi companies for ruthless exploitation and abuse.

The American ideal embraces the promise that economic progress can create an inclusive society in which prosperity is broadly shared. Work is more than simply a way to earn a living. It gives structure, dignity, and purpose to our lives.

Without robust policies and strong institutions, new innovations risk exacerbating the economic insecurity, political, and civil divides we are experiencing today. The question facing politicians now is about whether they took directions from Uber, Lyft, and other rideshare executives as a result of campaign contributions.

Again, revisit the Yes on Proposition 22 campaign in California, in which Uber, Lyft, and other gig companies donated millions of dollars to the Republican party, while the driver advocacy groups and unions raised a paltry amount. Uber, Lyft, and other gig companies eventually won the case.

The political overtone that followed the California Prop 5 debate was mind-boggling, to say the least. During the California Prop 5 debate, there were recriminations from both sides of the aisle, with acrimony that was really uncalled for. There were political outbursts at the bill as proof that "Republicans are the party of Uber" while "Democrats are the party of taxi cab unions." Maybe these outbursts should have been narrowed down to the "the party that supports exploitative slave-labor wages" and "the party that supports the right to decent livable wages," to live the American dream as guaranteed in our constitution.

There were some who attacked AB5 as part of a daily war on jobs. Really? War on jobs, or a war against slave-labor jobs? Do these drivers have the right to fight against a job that enslaves, dehumanizes, and robs them of the right to live the American dream? A job that studies have shown to cause untold miseries and mental problems that eventually resulted in suicide and homelessness?

At no time have the political parties—Republican, Democratic, Independent—shown any real desire to set aside their political differences and act in a concerted effort to address the issue of economic exploitation and abuse these drivers are subjected to by the rideshare digital taxi companies. If ever they showed any inclination to look into these issues, they did so perfunctorily. The inaction on the part of lawmakers to deal fairly and squarely with the uncompromising policies of digital taxi companies' lack of transparency, accountability, and fair wages has empowered them to create a market equivalent to that of slave-masters of the slavery era.

The protests and complaints signify a clarion call to act in a fair and just manner, with regulations that bring respect and dignity to their profession, just like any other profession. The issues are not political, to be decided on the basis of financial influence or political affiliation. These are our fellow citizens who work hard to live the American dream and need not be treated with disdain or as slaves.

In my opinion, the solution to protests across the nation and globally is simple and doesn't need to be decided contingent upon political affiliations, political contributions, and what have you. A fair and equitable solution could have been based on $1.20 per mile for a driver or a commission of, say, 30 percent of the rider's fare for digital taxi companies to enable rideshare drivers to meet their obligations—car notes, insurance, gas, repair and maintenance, depreciation—and leave something not fantastic but livable as a take-home wage. We must recognize that this is what they do for a living; this is what they do to send their children to school; this is what they do to pay for their mortgages and provide food and other life necessities for their families. They are gradually drowning and crying out for help, but they have been spurned. They are not protesting for the fun of it or out of sentiment. They are protesting because they are unjustly exploited and driven into abject poverty.

Why not look into the merits of their complaints, if for nothing else, for the sake of the American ideal, where every right of the human being is guaranteed without a dose of overbearing infringement or discrimination. It cannot be financially beneficial for a driver, it cannot be morally justified, it cannot be justified in any context other than sheer greed and horrendous abuse of power to offer a payment of $263 for a trip from Fresno, Texas, to Dallas, Texas.

Slavery was a lucrative economic institution embraced by many, but the evil of slavery was recognized by President Abraham Lincoln, who issued the Emancipation Proclamation on January 1, 1863. Women's voting rights, passed by Congress, June 4, 1919, and the Voting Rights Act of 1965, both took the courage and the integrity of enlightened leadership who saw the triumph of goodness and justice over evil as a virtue.

Maybe in years to come, there will emerge an administration and congress resolute and resolved to place the rights of these exploited, abused drivers and gig workers above campaign contributions and political affiliation. When did slave-masters ever disclose, with the idea of proportionate revenue sharing, without guidelines, the money they made from the sweat of their slaves? Never! There was no legal framework that limited the exploitation of slaves for unlimited financial gain. They had all the power and freedom on earth to exploit and abuse their slaves as they wished. Slaves had no right to negotiate for better working conditions, equitable income distribution, or human rights. This is exactly the condition rideshare drivers face in digital taxi platforms in the 21st-century economic system.

When did any rideshare company ever display the rider's fare or its claimed take rate (commission) on the driver's app to enable a driver to determine his earnings for a trip? Never! Uber unilaterally pays any amount to drivers, not related to a rider's fare. When the drivers disagree with the amount paid for a trip, Uber's defense is "You accepted the trip," implying that it has no intention, no obligation to pay what is right and appropriate. If this is 21st-century labor work philosophy, then other sectors of the economy, including governments, have the right not to consider pay raises for workers even when economic conditions dictate.

When drivers are robbed of their fair share of a rider's fare based on take rate (commission), are denied employee status, have no voice in wage negotiation, have no right to unionize, and have no legal protection against exploitative slave wages, then they can appropriately and rightly be classified as slave laborers.

All Made Possible

Rideshare companies are able to push through their exploitative policies and slave-labor agenda because of campaign contributions and lobbying to control and exploit a struggling group—mainly people of color, retirees and immigrants—ruthlessly for unlimited corporate financial gains. If the current trend of using political campaign contributions is a litmus test as to who gets what, then most of the civil rights and labor gains of the past centuries will be gradually eroded. Why? Because heavyweights are using their money to influence and silence the voice of justice when it matters most.

One day, as in the days of slavery, there will emerge a group of legislators—local, state, and federal—who will place a priority on the welfare of these groups and all citizens in general, ready and willing to act to right the wrongs of unjust exploitation. They will rise up and say, "This ain't right. This is morally wrong." They will be courageous and resolved to put forward a common legal framework for the industry to follow in order protect the rights of drivers and gig workers alike, putting an end to the unprecedented exploitation, abuse, and humiliation drivers are subjected to by rideshare companies.

One may argue in favor of doing business, but business practices that pay a pittance to the workers who give legitimacy to their business operations, treat them like rats in a cage, and a platform's algorithm to extort money from customers and drivers is absolute exploitation and slavery, not an economic model of prosperity and upward mobility. We need to call it what is.

CHAPTER 8

Labor Unions, Labor Organizers, Taxi Workers Alliances

The key to success and the road to ending the exploitation is to persevere. Perseverance will eventually overcome obstacles of injustice and pave the way for the rights of the oppressed. The relentless fight that the unions have embarked upon is commendable, and hopefully they will not cave under pressure. Labor unions, labor organizers, and drivers themselves must work indefatigably to resolve the issue of slave wages that rideshare companies work relentlessly to establish as the norm for drivers on their platform.

The chattel or the bondsmen of the rideshare companies are the rideshare drivers. Protests against the rideshare companies' model of exploitation seems to yield no appreciable results in an era when campaign contributions appear to be the deciding factor as to who gets what. These gig companies, in terms of campaign contributions, dwarf labor unions, labor organizers, taxi workers alliances, and other groups financially. They can raise huge sums of money in a few hours without affecting their profit margin, often by chipping away part of what they pay drivers. They can do surge pricing for customers if necessary to generate additional revenue. Employing these tactics nationwide gives them the ability to raise millions in a short period of time.

Labor unions, labor organizers, and taxi workers alliances do not have such leverage. This helps explain why rideshare companies remain uncompromising and unwilling to end their exploitation and abuse of drivers. It's like a financial war between the haves, with a big camp of wealthy supporters, and the have-nots, with no financial power but a reasonable circle of sympathizers. It's like a contest between an elephant and a rat. Change can come about when this contest turns out to be a contest like the one between the biblical David and Goliath.

Labor unions, labor organizers, and taxi workers alliances working together, with a planned vision and strategy, can in the long run turn things around and become a force in the political and economic arena. It will take putting heads together and harnessing the resources at their disposal judiciously to bring about positive change. Undoubtedly, one of the greatest human resources in the transportation service industry is the drivers, without which the industry would exist in name only. But managing and directing this human resource toward the attainment of a specific goal is a big problem. Beyond the daunting task of survival, painful sacrifices must be made to overcome ruthless exploitation for a better tomorrow.

The different organizations and the drivers themselves have to acknowledge that fighting for their rights is a worthwhile cause. This is what will bring out the best of those involved in this crusade for better planning and strategy. It will allow those involved to enter the realms of great ideas never dreamt of. Platforms do not provide service without drivers, and the power of drivers that has remained dormant for a long time needs to be activated in any way possible.

Instead of spending millions of dollars for a fight that produces nothing, strategy should focus on how to best invest substantial amounts of money to give drivers a greater share in the contemporary economy and set them up politically as a force to reckon with. Fortunately, there are newcomers in the rideshare business who may have a willingness to partner with the various labor groups and taxi workers alliances. Modalities favorable to all parties can be worked out, and this type of setup will provide enough drivers to handle supply and demand and consequently degrade the markets shares of those bent on exploiting drivers for wealth creation beneficial to themselves only.

All that is needed is a starting point focusing on creating a working partnership that gives dignity to all parties involved. Full- and part-time workers have to realize that being a part of a struggle that brings positive change is more rewarding than playing a subservient role in a business that offers no promise of economic prosperity and upward mobility. The right to be your authentic self and uplift others can only thrive in an atmosphere of mutual trust and respect, one that guarantees the dignity of all parties involved without undue exploitation and abuse of one party for financial gain.

Victory sometimes takes decades of agitation and protest,

but never give up in the middle of the fight. It is not life that matters most, but the courage you put to it and the legacy you leave.

A legacy of victory for drivers_____ ending the exploitation and abuse inherent in rideshare platforms, and derailing the reintroduction of slave market economic policy of the past era.

A legacy glorified in "YES WE CAN, BECAUSE WE CAN".

Printed in the United States
by Baker & Taylor Publisher Services